Sanity Savers

9 strategies for enjoying life for men living alone

Peter Mulraney

Copyright

ISBN-13: 978-1508444657

ISBN-10: 150844465X

Contents

Introduction

Being on your own, following the end of a long-term relationship, can be quite daunting. It often presents challenges, like boredom and loneliness.

My intention, in writing this book, is to introduce you to some strategies that will help you keep your sanity intact.

In what follows, I share seven strategies for finding constructive or interesting ways to use your alone time, and two personal growth and development strategies you can use to stay connected with the world, and to explore some of life's more intriguing questions.

These strategies will remind you that there are things you can do, things you can learn, places you can visit, and friends you can make. They also highlight the value of making commitments to your personal growth and engaging with others.

Over the last several years I have spent a fair amount of time on my own. My long-term relationship may not have ended when my wife accepted a position in another country, but it certainly changed form.

Since finding myself on my own for months at a time, I have employed the strategies I am sharing with you to write several books, focus on my spiritual journey, establish a blog, and stay connected to my extended family. I've also acquired a set of new skills, related to self-publishing and online marketing, had a lot of fun, met some interesting people, and travelled.

To be honest, I haven't had the time to feel bored or lonely.

I recommend that you explore some of the activities suggested in the first seven strategies. Discover which ones work for you and make the most of what they have to offer.

I encourage you to embrace strategies eight and nine: staying connected and befriending yourself. I believe these are essential for the ongoing sanity of anyone living alone.

Reading

You're reading this book, so I guess it's safe to assume you already know something about the value of reading. I know a lot of guys who read the paper, well at least the sports pages, and think that's all there is to reading. We're going a bit further than that.

In my experience, reading is one of the more enjoyable pastimes for someone living alone. It's not expensive, it can be done almost anywhere, and it's more active and engaging than watching TV, which the neuroscientists describe as a passive activity. If you want to keep your brain active and increase your chances of not getting dementia, reading is a better choice than TV, simply because you need to use active imagination when you read. If you're not quite sure what that means, consider that what you see on the TV is always someone else's visual interpretation of the story - whether you're watching the history channel or the news. When you're reading the story in words, you get to dream up your own visual interpretation or mental pictures of the words, based on your unique perspective of the world. That's the bit that exercises your brain cells.

Reading is an activity that can be done for several different reasons, which we'll explore in the following sections.

Reading for entertainment

This is the world of fiction or storytelling. There is an ever-increasing supply of stories for you to choose from, so you'll never run out of books to read. There are books for every imaginable interest.

Go to any brick and mortar or online bookstore and just look at the list of categories. Okay, you might not be into romance or erotica or that vampire paranormal stuff, but there are stacks of other categories to choose from: crime, mysteries, thrillers, action-hero, espionage, historical-fiction, fantasy, science-fiction, war stories and literary masterpieces to name a few. And, they all have sub-genres or sub-categories with thousands of authors to choose from.

I'd also include biographies and autobiographies in this section, not that I am suggesting that they are works of fiction, but because we read them more for their entertainment value than for any other reason - a form of voyeurism.

If you haven't ventured beyond the papers or the self-help section in recent years, do yourself a favour, and buy yourself a novel, or go to your local library and borrow one or two.

If you need a place to start, try one of my Inspector West novels, a Chief Inspector Gamache novel by Louise Penny, or a Roy Grace novel by Peter James.

Reading for information

Another reason to read is to find information. This is the world of non-fiction, where you can go to get help or find out about those things that interest you. This book is in this category.

This is where you find the history books and the how-to books, shelved with the cooking books and the art and craft books, along with all the political science and real science books.

There is some fascinating material to be found in this part of the library or bookstore. If you want to know something about Islam or Buddhism or Christianity, or the history of warfare, or how they get the retina display on an iPad, or to discover who was behind the global financial crisis, this is the place. There will be a book here for you, no matter what you're interested in.

This is also the place to find information on setting up a business, money management, along with ideas on time management and all sorts of ways you can be more productive. It's also where you'll find all those 'how-to-get-rich-quick' books, which seem to be multiplying like rabbits after a good rain.

Despite the danger, this is one of my favourite parts of the bookstore. This is where you can find thought-provoking books like: *The Black Swan* by Nassin Nicholas Taleb; *The Master Strategist* by Ketan J Patel; and *Hot, Flat and Crowded* by Thomas L Friedmann.

Reading for inspiration

Some times you simply need a lift. Fortunately, there are books that can help you get through it when you're down.

When you're pondering the meaning of life, or wondering why you're here, and what you're supposed to be doing with yourself, there are books to help with that too.

The thing to remember is that you are not alone on the planet, even if you are alone at home. There are others who are treading the same path or who have gone before you, and some of them have written about their experiences and what they learnt along the way.

We like to think that we have original ideas, unique questions or personal moments that no-one else could possibly understand. But when we engage with fellow pilgrims, we discover that we were mistaken in our belief.

When I was much younger, I started in this part of the bookstore with Wayne Dyer, before moving on to Richard Rohr, Osho, John O'Donohue, Deepak Chopra and Paul Ferrini, to name a few of the authors in this part of my library.

In 2014 I added my own contribution to this library - *Sharing the Journey: Reflections of a Reluctant Mystic*.

Format: books, e-books and blogs

Once upon a time, we were restricted to reading paper based books, magazines, comics and newspapers. You can still read the paper version, but now you can choose an electronic version for many titles.

The advent of the e-book, in particular, has changed the reading experience for anyone with an e-reader device, tablet computer or smartphone. Not only are e-books a lot cheaper to buy, you don't have to worry about having the shelf space to store them either. Amazon, Apple or Kobo, or any of the other online stores, will store them in the cloud for you, to access from anywhere at anytime and, of course, you can store a copy on your device to read without having to be online.

I do most of my reading these days on my iPad, even the books I buy from Amazon or Kobo. All you need is the app for your device. I have a couple of Kindles, one from my pre-iPad days and a newer Kindle Paper White, that was a gift, so even when the iPad is recharging I still have a device to read on, and they all seem to know which page I'm up to, provided I turn them on within range of a wireless router.

Despite having all those e-readers, there are still times when I like to read paper based books. There is something about that experience you just don't get with an e-book. Besides, I have a library with a few thousand printed titles that I like to revisit. There is something about sitting in a room full of books that you just can't capture with an electronic library of hundreds of titles stored in the cloud, or on that device in your hand.

On the other hand, if you're someone who changes apartments frequently or who travels, an e-book based library makes a lot of sense. Another thing I like about e-books is that if I see a book I want to read at two am in the morning, I can buy it on the spot and start reading without leaving my chair. It can take up to two or three weeks for a paperback to arrive in Australia from Amazon or the Book Depository, and there aren't any local bookshops open at that hour where I live.

The electronic world has also brought us the world of blogging, which provides online magazines or journals written by people like you and me, on any topic you can think of, which you can read for free if you have internet access. You can find a blog on any topic simply by asking Google or any other search engine for: 'your topic' blogs.

Blogs provide readers with an opportunity to interact with writers. If you want to say something about the content of a blog post or article, you simply add a comment. If you find a blog you really enjoy, you can sign up to have the content delivered to your email inbox.

Just reading through the stream of comments is often as much fun as reading the blog post itself.

The online library

If you want to do some study, there are hundreds of courses available online.

Check out openculture.com for details on some of the more serious university offerings.

Fortunately, there are other options for those of us who are just interested in finding out about stuff. We can turn to YouTube and Vimeo, two places with lots of video presentations on a range of interesting topics.

If you're interested in short, thought-provoking presentations, try Ted talks.

If you prefer PowerPoint presentations, check out what's available on SlideShare.net.

If you don't mind paying a few dollars for a course, see what interests you over at Udemy.com.

There is something else you can do in the online library that they don't encourage in your local library: you can discuss books with other readers. One place you can do this is at Goodreads.com, which allows you to join groups based on interest or book categories, where you will find other readers discussing the books. Another book club site is Shelfari.com.

Resources

Online courses

Open Culture: http://www.openculture.com

Udemy: https://www.udemy.com

Online presentations

Ted Talks: http://www.ted.com/talks

YouTube: https://www.youtube.com

Vimeo: https://vimeo.com

SlideShare: http://www.slideshare.net

Online book clubs

GoodReads: http://www.goodreads.com

Shelfari: http://www.shelfari.com

supplies. And, remember, you're the only person who needs to be able to read it. Often, it's the act of writing that does the work, and maybe you'll never reread what you write. There are plenty of pages in my journals I have trouble reading, so heaven help anyone who stumbles across them when I'm gone.

If you're not sure how to get started, purchase journals with a daily question, reflection or a theme, like a gratitude journal, where you buy books or from one of the many online sites that support journaling.

You can also use a journal to record your insights and responses to questions and exercises you find in self-development or personal growth books.

I promise you'll learn more about life and yourself from journaling than you ever will watching TV.

Diaries

A diary is a specific type of journal used for recording the events of your day. In a diary you simply create a record of what happened. Once you cross the line into reflecting on what happened, or why certain events occurred in the course of your journey, you've crossed over into creating a journal or the work of self-discovery. There is nothing wrong with that. Moving from diary to journal is actually quite common.

Letter writing

If blogging, which is like writing a letter to the world, is not your cup of tea, maybe old style letter writing is something you can revisit. We may live in a world of instant communication but people still appreciate the thought you put into a handwritten letter.

Although letter writing seems to have become a dying art-form, thanks to email and, more recently, social media, it still has it's place.

I notice that people still write letters to the editor. You could do that if you're into reading the paper. You could make that a weekly or daily activity if you're seriously into current affairs, although be warned, a lot of that is done by email these days.

Then there are all those people in your life that perhaps you haven't seen in a while, who might appreciate a letter or a card letting them know that you're thinking about them. Postage is still inexpensive, which is one reason why the postal services are going broke.

If you're feeling civic, maybe you could send your local politician a few ideas or join a letter writing campaign to raise awareness of issues in your local community.

Exercising

There are many reasons for exercising, most of them related to fitness and wellbeing but, in our context, exercise is one of those activities you can devote time to on a regular basis.

Taken seriously, exercise can consume hours of your time, but there is no need to take it to those levels, at least initially. Not everyone is destined to be an Olympic Athlete or a Masters' Champion.

Anyone can exercise. Some forms are easy and inexpensive, and everyone benefits from regular exercise.

If you haven't exercised for a while, you might want to check with your doctor before you take on anything strenuous. Another word of warning before you begin, start slowly and gradually increase your work rate over time.

Rushing into exercise, of any type, with enthusiasm is a painful experience for the muscles, and results in a lot of people giving up before they really begin.

Walking, jogging and skipping

You know how to walk but, if you're like the rest of us, you've been driving the car, catching the subway and taking the elevator. That's okay. I do those things, too.

A gentle way of easing yourself into walking is to put on some loose fitting clothes and your sneakers, or any other soft-soled shoes, and go for a ten to twenty minute walk in the evening, or morning if you're an early riser.

If you live near a park or a river, they are great places to walk. If you don't, go for a walk around the block, or up and down the street, and see what's going on in your neighbourhood from street level.

If you find that walking isn't exciting enough, get some decent cross-trainers or running shoes and start jogging. This one requires a bit more commitment, at least three times a week, but daily is even better. I was a runner in my youth but I confess to slowing down - now I walk.

Walking and jogging are two activities that lend themselves to being done in groups. Exercising with a friend or two is a way to make it a habit, and it gives you an opportunity to talk as you exercise together.

Sometimes the weather is against you when it comes to either walking or jogging. This is where skipping comes in. All you need is a skipping rope and a space to turn it. Skipping might be a simple exercise, but as with all the others, show it some respect and work your way into it gradually, otherwise you will end up sore. Skipping is a bit like jogging on the spot, and it's good for the abs too - all that shaking up and down tightens those belly muscles.

Swimming

If you want to give your body a bit more of a total workout, consider swimming. Don't know how to swim? They teach adults. Look up adult swimming classes in your local area with Google or any other search engine.

This is another form of exercise that takes time. When you get into swimming laps to increase your fitness, you can easily spend an hour at the pool. Swimming is a fairly solitary pursuit, unless you join a club. There are social and competitive swimming clubs. Ask at your local pool.

Cycling

There are several levels at which you can tackle cycling, and there is a large range of cycles or bikes available to choose from. See the Wikipedia link in resources for more details.

For our purposes we'll consider stationary cycles and road bikes.

Stationary cycles are the exercise machines you generally find in gyms, which you can also buy for home use if you don't have access to a gym, or don't want to join one. A stationary or exercise bike gives you all the exercise without any of the dangers of riding on the road, or any of the worries about riding in rain or heat.

Road bikes are designed for riding on urban streets and dedicated cycle or bike paths. This is the type you are probably familiar with, from either your childhood or from having kids.

As with walking or jogging, cycling is an activity that you can either do alone or in groups. You've no doubt seen groups of cyclists on the roads, and sitting in or around coffee shops. From my observations, cycling seems to be a weekend activity for many people.

In fact, you can join touring groups that go for day or weekend tours of the countryside. Joining such groups allows you to make new friends and fill up a whole day or weekend having fun, instead of sitting home navel gazing, and wondering what to do with yourself. You can even go on bike tours in other parts of the country or in overseas locations. Imagine yourself spending hours training and then enjoying a whole week, or longer, exploring another place with a group of like-minded people.

This is another activity you'll need to spend money on if you don't own a bike. You don't have to buy a top of the range carbon fibre bike for thousands of dollars. You can still get a serviceable bike for a few hundred dollars, or less, if you go for a used bike from your local cycling store, or from eBay or similar sites.

You can always trade up later, if you fall in love with cycling, and that's when you can think about the lycra and the fancy shoes. Until then, you can comfortably cycle in street clothes and sneakers. You see people doing that all the time. There's even a lad in my neighbourhood that flies past me on his bike wearing a suit, when I'm walking to the bus stop on my way to the office.

If your bike hasn't been used for a while, like years, it will probably need new tyres and a service before you take it out on the road.

Bicycle maintenance is another skill you can spend time mastering along the way.

Yoga and Pilates

These are exercises you can do indoors with a minimum of equipment. The basic requirement is an exercise mat and some loose fitting clothes. No special shoes required, you can do these exercises barefoot.

It's probably best to go to classes to learn how to do either of these, but you can teach yourself the basic moves using DVD or on-line courses, or an instruction book. The advantage of starting by going to classes is the commitment required to establish the exercise habit. Use Google or any other search engine to find out what's available in your area.

Don't be fooled by the apparent ease of either of these exercise regimes. Some of the exercises can be pretty strenuous, and many require a lot of practice before you'll feel comfortable doing them.

Once you get a basic routine under your belt, you can easily spend thirty minutes to an hour each day on these exercises.

Pilates is still on my list of things to start. I've got the book and the exercise mat.

The gym

Recently, I listened to a discussion on gym membership on WYNC, my favourite New York radio station, which was exploring the monthly subscription business model used in the industry. Most people sign up, pay monthly and don't go. So a word of warning. Don't sign up unless you know you will actually go. You will be better off paying the casual rate, until you're in a position to make an informed decision based on your actual attendance. Keep a written record to establish your attendance pattern. Apparently, most people lie to themselves about how often they go to the gym once they have signed up.

If you're looking to work with a personal trainer or work with weights, the gym is the place to go. If you're simply looking to increase your general level of fitness, without getting seriously into weights, you could consider setting up a gym at home. There are a lot of exercises you can do using your body weight. Simply look up that topic with Google or your search engine of choice, or check the link below in resources. If you live in an apartment building with a gym, that you already pay for in your rent, you already have a home gym. All you have to do is use it.

Sleeping

Activity is one side of the exercise coin. The other is sleeping.

Most of us know that we turn into grumpy old men if we don't get sufficient sleep. There is no need to deny yourself sleep just because you'll be sleeping on your own. So instead of staying up late watching TV, go to bed and get a good night's sleep.

Not only will a lack of sleep make you grumpy, there's plenty of evidence (which you can read online if you need to convince yourself - ask our friend Google about sleep deprivation) that not getting enough sleep leads to things like:

- Reduced alertness

Growing things

I'll start with a confession. I live in a suburban house with both a front and back garden. Quite a few of the images on my blog are photographs of plants in those gardens. But, to be honest, although I enjoy gardening, I have a gardener, who spends a couple of hours every second week maintaining them. I also live in a part of the world where it does not snow, so we can enjoy our gardens year round, provided we can keep up the watering required to help the plants get through the hot, dry Australian summer - and, fortunately, someone invented automated irrigation systems to take care of that.

A few of my neighbours, who do not have gardeners, spend most of their weekends in their gardens. A garden is a place where you can either spend hours working in it or a place where you can spend hours enjoying doing some of the other activities I've mentioned, like reading, drawing, painting, photography, exercise or simply meditating.

Gardening may not take up a lot of your time, but it's an activity you can include in your daily or weekly schedule, along with whatever else you choose to do to enjoy your hours with yourself.

Herbs, vegetables and flowers

My current gardens are in the category referred to as aesthetic. I have a couple of fruit trees and grow a few herbs, in pots, but most of the plant life is there for looking at.

Some of my friends have extensive vegetable gardens - one of the side benefits of being connected to an Italian community.

If you have the space, you can grow a lot of your own fruit and vegetables, or like one of my older, retired friends, with an extensive and productive garden, you can supply your family and friends, especially over the summer.

If you live in the suburbs, you can do more than mow the grass every week or so.

The indoor garden

Gardening is not restricted to the outdoors in temperate climates. You can also become an indoor gardener, using pot plants or hydroponics to grow a range of vegetables. Many of the vegetables you buy at the supermarket these days are grown using hydroponics.

You can find out how it all works by asking Google or any other search engine, or by following the link to what Wikipedia has on the topic in the resources section below.

Start with a few pots or a small hydroponics kit, unless you're intending to convert your shed into an urban farm.

Community gardens

Another way of getting into gardening is to become part of a community garden.

A community garden generally involves a group of people growing things on a shared piece of land. In some parts of the world, this may involve establishing a garden on an abandoned allotment. In other places, City Councils or individuals make a piece of land available for people living in a neighbourhood to grow food.

You can find a community garden in your area using your favourite search engine, or you can start one. Either way, you'll get to meet people and spend time out of the house.

For more details, follow the link to the Wikipedia article on community gardens in the resources section.

Taking care of public spaces

If you're not into growing things, there is one other 'gardening' option you can consider, which I understand is popular with people in some parts of the world: taking care of public spaces. Query your search engine on that topic, to see what other people are doing around the world to take care of their public spaces.

On a local level, this can simply mean adopting a street or part of a park, for example, and spending a few hours each week removing litter. You get to spend a few hours doing something and the world is left a better place that day. And you never know, if others see you cleaning up your adopted space they might even stop littering, because they know someone cares about the place. They even have a name for this approach to public engagement - the broken windows theory.

Another thing to keep in mind about public gardens is that they are microcosms of nature, places you can go to recharge your spirit.

secular organisations as well, like Meals on Wheels, for example, which delivers food to homebound and elderly people, that you can look into joining. And let's face it, these days, no-one is going to reject your service based on your religious persuasion if you volunteer to help out.

Local community

Another option for spending some time in service is volunteering to do things for people in your local community. Perhaps you could read to people in the local aged-care facility or simply visit an older person to chat.

Are there people in your street or building that need help with their shopping, cleaning or some other task, like getting to an appointment? Not everyone can afford to hire help, and not everyone is ordering home delivery online. Some don't know how. Maybe you can show them how it's done or do it for them.

You could volunteer to participate in any senior citizen service programs provided by your local City Council. In my area, for example, they are always looking for someone to drive the community bus or join the graffiti removal squad. Or, instead of caring for public spaces on your own, join a local land-care or conservation group.

All or any of these options will get you out of the house and mixing with other people.

Family

Another group you can serve is your family, especially if they live in the same town or city. Some family time will be social, but there will be times when family members appreciate a helping hand. If you have grandchildren, offer to be the babysitter while the young parents have a night out or go away for the weekend. If you like gardening, maybe you can be the gardener your kids, brother, sister or parents, can't afford.

Maybe you don't need to visit an aged care facility to spend time with a lonely older person - you could simply spend some time with your parents or widowed mother. If they live out of town, consider getting them onto to Skype or a similar service. If my 85 year old mother can use it, yours probably can too, and you can spend time chatting and seeing how they are, instead of watching TV.

Travel

They claim that a change is as good as a holiday. Well, let me tell you that a holiday beats a change - every time.

If you have the funds, overseas travel is worth the effort. If you don't have a lot of money, travel locally. My mother, for example, goes on what we boys refer to as 'seniors tours'. Basically, interstate or local bus tours with a few overnight stays costing a few hundred dollars, as opposed to the thousands you'll need for a decent overseas tour.

These days you can organise your own travel itinerary and book all your flights and accommodation online, or you can choose to have a travel agent to do it all for you. You can travel around on your own or join an organised tour.

In places where I don't speak the language, I prefer to go with an organised tour, unless I know someone in country who is happy to show me around. I had a fun experience in Romania, where I had a friend who helped me buy a train ticket in Bucharest - a one-way ticket was all you could buy, mind you. When I needed to buy the ticket for the return leg, I encountered a middle-aged woman who didn't speak a word of English. There was a lot of laughter, as I negotiated using the only word in Romanian I knew - Bucuresti - so at least she knew where I wanted to go, and I found the word for Tuesday in the phrases in the Lonely Planet guide. At least with the money all I had to do was show her the notes.

One thing I can report from my travels is that most people are friendly. You won't get to meet them if you stay home.

When I go to Italy, I stay in apartments, which you can book online, and travel around on the trains on my own, because I speak the language. Another reason to study a foreign language or two. In fact, the last time I was in New York, I found myself speaking Italian in Penn Station, to two young travellers looking for the train to JFK airport, so you never know when a foreign language will come in handy.

Don't let anyone convince you that they speak English all over the world. They might in the hotels servicing tourists, but don't count on it, and if you want to get out and experience mixing with the locals, they'll appreciate the effort you made to learn a few words in their language.

If foreign languages aren't your thing that is no reason not to travel. There are plenty of English speaking countries to visit. Australia might be a long way from anywhere, except New Zealand, but it's a great place to visit, it's a lot bigger than most people think, and most of us are friendly.

Search for tours and travel destinations online or visit a travel agent and start planning.

Catch up with friends

You might be living alone but you don't have to be a hermit. Just because your long-term relationship with your wife or partner is over, doesn't mean you're cut off from everybody else.

Make it a point to catch up with your friends for a meal or coffee, on a regular basis. If all your friends were 'her' friends, get out and join some groups so you can make new friends of your own. You're not the only lonely guy on the planet, or in your neighbourhood.

By joining groups or doing courses you can meet people with similar interests. All you have to do is be brave enough to ask questions, and remember, the easiest way to start a conversation is to encourage people to talk about themselves.

Go to the game instead of sitting with the box

Do you follow a football team, or any sports team, for that matter? Instead of watching the big game home alone, why not treat yourself, every now and then, by actually going to the game.

If you hate huge crowds, find a team in a local league or competition you can follow. That's another way you can meet people and, as I mentioned in the service chapter, local teams are always looking for supporters who can do more that simply attend games.

Staying connected

Some of us are introverts with a tendency to isolate ourselves. Others are extroverts and love nothing more than interacting with people. If you're with the extroverts, you can probably skip this - you already know how to stay connected.

But if you belong to the other group, or have tendencies in that direction, read on, because you probably need a gentle push to move you out of your comfort zone.

Most of us have a comfort zone, or group of behaviours, we prefer to stay with. A lot of us are resistant to change, and we withdraw into ourselves to cope with significant changes in our life situation. Losing your partner to death or divorce can be one of those devastating experiences, when all you want is to be left alone, to grieve. I understand that, but you can't stay there. That's a lonely, desolate place.

If you're feeling stuck in that desolate place, reach out to people who love you. If there is no one there for you to turn to, reach out for support through groups like Beyond

Blue or Befrienders Worldwide. I don't want to be overly dramatic, but the statistics for suicide include a lot of guys who were not able to move on from the loss of their partner, and their subsequent loneliness. I'm here to remind you that you have other options, and some of them are as easy as picking up the phone to call a friend.

Family

I'm part of a large extended family based around my birth family and in-laws. I come from a family of ten, so when we have family gatherings we often have quite a crowd.

I have different relationships with each of my siblings, and each of my in-laws. I even get along with my mother-in-law. I spend more time with some of them than with others. But we always have a good time when we are together as a group, even when we are attending a funeral.

One of the rowdiest gatherings we have each year is a cousins' dinner, with my wife's cousins and all our kids. This often starts in a restaurant and ends in one of our homes.

Families are great for giving support. I'm only on my own for those months of the year that make up the American school year, minus the one or two I spend in New York, but members of my extended family are always including me in things or asking me over for a meal.

Why am I sharing this? To remind you that whatever family you have, they can be a great source of support.

If you have children with young families of their own, remember that you're still a grandfather, and grandchildren can give you hours of enjoyment. Don't cut yourself off from their love and adoration. They will grow up soon enough.

Friends

Beyond your family circle, you probably have a group of friends. These are the guys you grew up with, the guys you played sport with, the guys you work with, and the guys that see through all your bullshit.

They're also the guys you can talk things through with. Given the state of today's world, you're probably not the only one in your group who has experienced the end of a long-term relationship. Friends are there for each other. Some times they are there for you and other times you're there for them. So stay in touch. These are the guys who will remind you that life goes on, even after and through difficult experiences.

Do things with your friends. Take a course together, learn a foreign language and travel, join a service club, or exercise together. Go out on the town together. It's a lot more fun than doing it on your own.

Neighbours

Often, we don't live next door to family and friends, but we do live next door to our neighbours.

When you live alone, it's a good idea to befriend at least some of your neighbours, especially if you're in poor health or don't have many family or other visitors.

Interacting with your neighbours is a way of making friends, but it's also a way of creating a network of people who look out for each other. Whether you like it or not, your neighbours notice your comings and goings and lack there of, just as you notice theirs. That could come in handy in a health emergency, and a neighbour is more likely to come straight away, if they know who you are when you call them for help.

Something else to consider is giving someone that you trust a key to your house or apartment, so that the neighbours, the police or ambulance crew, don't have to break the door in during an emergency.

Pets

If you find that you just don't like being home alone, consider getting yourself a pet. Walking the dog can be a great form of exercise but caring for a goldfish or two can also be rewarding.

Just remember that pets equal responsibility, and they cost money. There is a lot more to looking after a cat or dog than buying it food.

Do some research before you commit yourself to picking up dog shit for the next ten to fifteen years.

Maybe the goldfish option is not such a silly idea after-all.

New relationships

There are a lot of women out there living alone as well. Statistically, more women end up on their own following the death of their spouse than men. For some mysterious reason, they still seem to live longer than we do.

For every divorced man there is a divorced woman out there, somewhere. And, believe it or not, there are some women who have even chosen to stay single, and others who have put off entering into a long-term relationship because they haven't found the right guy, yet.

The interesting thing is that while many older single guys are looking for a new long-term partner, a lot of the girls are looking for something else. Some of this is driven by the differing expectations society has of men and women.

Men tend to get their freedom in their youth, and then settle down to become responsible, conservative citizens as they get older. Some get so conservative they turn into grumpy old men, but it seems even grumpy old men like to be cuddled.

Women on the other hand, often find themselves locked into the expectation of being a responsible wife and mother, until they move beyond childbearing age. This is when many women discover who they are, and walk away from existing relationships. Yes, despite all the Hollywood hype, it's the women who are instigating most divorces.

A woman released from a relationship, and all its expectations, by death or divorce, often finds herself free enough to be her own person for the first time in her life, even though she may be fifty, sixty or seventy. And, she's not likely to be looking for another relationship in a hurry.

Many liberated women are not interested in looking after another man, especially a grumpy old one.

Sure, there will be some who want another long-term relationship, but don't count on meeting them where you hang out with the boys.

These days there are all sorts of relationships, and maybe you'll need to consider options other than the traditional one if you want a new partner.

If you want a new relationship, you'll need to get out of the house and go meet people. But don't rush into it. You need to give yourself time to recover from the end of your last relationship, before launching into another one with the first woman you meet. The statistics on rebound relationships aren't that encouraging either.

There are websites for finding people looking for new relationships. I can't recommend any simply because I haven't used any, but I'm sure our friend Google can help you with that, or ask your friends, especially those that have found themselves a new partner or love interest.

I know some wonderful couples that have come together after the ending of previous long-term relationships. Some of them have moved in together, while others spend time together but live in their own spaces.

A new relationship is a possibility, but you need to keep in mind that it's not the only possible or probable outcome. Many of us will end up on our own at the end of a long-term relationship, and that means embracing the reality of living alone.

Resources

Support groups

Befrienders Worldwide: http://www.befrienders.org

Beyond Blue: http://www.beyondblue.org.au

Choosing a pet

http://www.wikihow.com/Choose-a-Pet

Befriending yourself

For your entire life, you have been living with the best friend you could ever have - yourself. Unfortunately, most of us have lived our lives totally oblivious to that fact, and so, when we are on our own, we feel lonely. Some of us actually treat ourselves as the enemy.

It doesn't have to be that way.

One of the possible outcomes of living alone is finding out who you really are. I say one of the possible outcomes deliberately, because there are others, and you need to make a deliberate choice to embark on a journey of self-discovery.

I encourage you to make that choice, simply because the alternatives, like loneliness, depression and alcoholism, are not all that enjoyable. And suicide is final - you don't get to reconsider it after the fact, at least not in this dimension.

Self-discovery

The external world is the focus of most of our attempts to understand the world and our place in it. It's true, there is a lot of interesting stuff in the world we can study, and we can keep ourselves busy for hours doing precisely that, as I have indicated in earlier chapters. In fact, you can hide there if you choose.

The journey of self-discovery, on the other hand, is an inner journey, which can be a very interesting, revealing, and surprising experience, as you encounter yourself along the way. You'll definitely discover that you are not who you currently think you are, if you undertake the trip.

Reluctant mystics, like me, have been on this pathway, off and on, for most of our lives, so I can introduce you to a few friends and techniques to help you undertake the journey of self discovery, or as I often see it, the journey of self-recovery.

To make this journey, you need to turn your focus away from studying things outside yourself and start studying yourself. This journey is about noticing what's going on in your life and wondering why.

If you were divorced after ten or more years of marriage, instead of feeling angry, shocked or betrayed, recognise that as an event you could notice, and wonder why it happened. And, here's my first pointer: never wonder why anything happened to you but always wonder why it happened for you to notice. Ever wondered why some things appear again and again in your life? They keep happening until you notice whatever the hidden lesson is. That's why some guys end up being divorced multiple times.

What does it tell you about the person you have been presenting to the world, if the woman that you claim you love decided to leave you? I never said this was going to be either easy or comfortable, at least in the early days, but if you really want to befriend yourself, you have to be honest with yourself. That means shining a light on all those lies you tell yourself about yourself, and everybody else in your life, including the ones who have died.

This journey is not something you'll complete in an afternoon or by attending a weekend workshop. This journey requires commitment to ongoing exploration.

I suggest you start by learning to simply stop and check in with yourself, and, in my experience, the best way to achieve that is through meditation.

Meditation

One of the first steps on the road to self-recovery is slowing down, and learning to sit and do nothing.

This is a major challenge for a lot of us. We've grown up in a society where we were encouraged to keep ourselves busy. In fact, a lot of us are actually addicted to activity, or our devices, and don't ever give ourselves any down time. Even when you're doing nothing in particular there is a voice in your head, that sounds a lot like your father's, mother's, some teacher's from your childhood, or, heaven forbid, your ex-wife's, telling you that you should be doing something.

That voice has been driving your decision making for as long as you can remember, and it will continue to do so until you tell it who's in charge.

Meditation is the first step to getting to that point.

When I first started looking into meditation, I was under the misperception that it was a religious activity. It can be, but it doesn't have to be.

The type of meditation I practice these days is called Mindfulness Meditation. It may have its roots in Buddhist practices, but you don't have to take on any beliefs to practise it. *Waking Up: Searching for Spirituality without Religion*, written by Sam Harris, a scientist, philosopher and famous skeptic, is an interesting read if you're interested in that perspective.

If you're particularly religious, you can follow a meditation practice aligned with your religion - they all have one - because all practices lead to the same place in the end.

The simplest form of meditation that I know is something you can try right now. Put the book down, sit comfortably in a chair, close your eyes, and just notice your breathing. Focus your attention on your breath and let any thoughts that come into your awareness float by, like clouds in the sky of your mind. If you realise you have chased a thought down a rabbit hole, simply bring your awareness back to your breathing. When you've had enough, slowly open your eyes and bring your attention back into the room.

When you first start meditating you may find it difficult to sit still for even ten minutes at a time. Some people go to sleep well before ten minutes are up. Don't panic, and don't give up if that happens to you. It's fairly normal. If you snore, you'll wake yourself up, eventually - I did.

Start with ten minutes, and gradually increase the amount of time you meditate up to twenty or thirty minutes. Many teachers recommend meditating for twenty minutes two times a day.

You can set the timer on your smartphone to remind you when the time is up. A gentle chime works best.

Meditation needs to become an ongoing practice if you are seriously interested in befriending yourself.

There is a wealth of material, online and in bookstores, on meditation that you can tap into, and there are many meditation centres around the world where you can learn to meditate.

One of the books I find helpful is: *Wherever You Go There You Are* by Jon Kabat-Zinn.

Journal work

For some reason, journaling works best if you use a pen and paper, so get yourself a decent exercise book or visual diary, if you like to doodle and draw as well as write.

You can start journaling by asking yourself some questions and then simply writing down whatever answer comes up. The secret is not to think about it too much or to edit what you write. Just write - sometimes the answers really surprise you.

A few starter questions:

- What do I believe in?

- What could I live without?

- What can't I live without?

- What hurts am I holding on to?

- What do I want to do with my life?

- What are my special talents and qualities?

- How do I feel about (a specific event or person)?

- Why did (a specific event or person) show up in my life?

When you want to go a bit deeper, consider forgiving everyone in your life for all the hurts you have experienced.

Then consider forgiving yourself for all the hurts you have imagined.

Journal work can be challenging, so it might pay to work with some guidelines from others who have gone before us. A few books that I found useful are:

- *Your Ultimate Life Plan* by Jennifer Howard

- *Change Your Thoughts, Change Your Life* by Wayne Dyer

- *Real Happiness* by Paul Ferrini, and

- *Love is letting go of fear* by Jerry Jampolsky.

Another approach to journal work is to write out the story of your life. You don't have to share it with anyone but yourself. We're all carrying around the story of everything that has ever happened to us - the good, the bad, and the ugly things. Using a journal is one way of getting in touch with that story.

One resource for really getting in touch with your story is *Writing from the heart* by Nancy Aronie. I participated in one of her workshops in New York. Interestingly, most of the people doing the workshop were single women using writing as therapy to uncover their stories. It was an amazing experience.

Use this information to get started on journaling, but be aware that there is a lot more help available in the online library: just type 'journaling' into your search engine of choice.

One journaling activity I recommend is keeping a gratitude journal - a book in which you write down all the people and things in your life that you are grateful for. A list you can add to, and turn to on those days when you're feeling down.

Resources

Books

Wherever You Go There You Are by Jon Kabat-Zinn

Your Ultimate Life Plan by Jennifer Howard

Change Your Thoughts, Change Your Life by Wayne Dyer

Real Happiness by Paul Ferrini.

Writing from the heart by Nancy Aronie.

Journals with prompts to get you started

Soulful Journals: http://www.soulfuljournals.com

Summary

On our journey together, we have covered nine strategies for maintaining your sanity while living alone.

The first seven strategies: reading, writing, learning a new skill, exercising, growing things, serving and having fun, are about finding constructive ways to occupy your time. Many of us are good at doing things, so I hope you found some things you can investigate or embrace as fulfilling pastimes. I also hope you'll have the courage to step out and challenge yourself to learn something new. It's a lot of fun - I've certainly learnt a lot about publishing and internet marketing since I decided to write a book, and it's been really interesting as well, especially for someone who was never ever going to be on FaceBook or Twitter.

The importance of the last two strategies: staying connected and befriending yourself, cannot be overstated. These are the two things that, in my humble opinion, will enable you to continue to enjoy life on your own.

There is a vast difference between being lonely and being alone. The choice to befriend yourself will help you appreciate that difference. It's a choice I encourage you to take.

The alternatives are nowhere near as enjoyable and all of them are detrimental to your sanity.

My purpose in writing this book was to put a resource into your hands so that you had somewhere to start. I'm sure that there are many other things you could do other than what I have suggested, but sometimes you need a little nudge to get you started.

I hope I've given you that nudge.

Peter Mulraney

Adelaide 2015

About the author

Peter Mulraney lives in Adelaide, Australia. With a passion for sharing knowledge and explaining things, he has written instructional and procedural material in the fields of banking, education and government.

He is the author of the Inspector West series of crime/romance novels, which explore the lives of people who commit crimes, mess up relationships and fall in love - not necessarily in that order - and the life of Inspector West, who sometimes solves a crime or two.

He is also the author of *Sharing the Journey: Reflections of a Reluctant Mystic*, exploring the journey of life, which we are all participating in - consciously or unconsciously.

The Living Alone series is based on Peter's experience of living on his own.

You can keep up with Peter by:

- following his blog at www.petermulraney.com

- interacting with him on his FacebookPage www.facebook.com/petermulraney.author, or

- at amazon.com/author/petermulraney.

Other titles by author

Thank You

Thank you for purchasing *Sanity Savers*.

If you found it useful please tell your friends and associates and, if you have a moment to spare, leave a short review on Amazon.

As you may be aware, reader reviews give a book social validation and encourage others to read it, so your help in spreading the word is gratefully appreciated.

Peter Mulraney

CPSIA information can be obtained at www.ICGtesting.com
Printed in the USA
LVOW10s1430260416

485401LV00003B/164/P